Gone From Sight:

Time To Grieve!

Gone From Sight: Time To Grieve

Published by M. Johnson and MJ2 Coaching, Boston, Massachusetts

Published May 2023

Printed in the United States.

ISBN: 978-1-312-58822-6

Gone From Sight:
Time To Grieve!

Introduction

Life is unpredictable and stressful.

Condolences to you and your family!

The unfortunate truth is that death is a part of life. Knowing this does not make it feel better.

Your grief process is unique and not linear. There are 5 general stages of grief. The phases you will learn in this workbook. Please know that phases can overlap, return out of order, arise without warning, betriggered by a situation, and or co-exist.

Professional grief counseling is strongly recommended.

Grief can consume us and is hard to process. It may be hard to find comfort in what occurred and you are hurting. If you need support, please call SAMHSA's National Helpline at 1 (800) 662-4357 or NAMI at 1 (800) 950-6264.

You are not alone, though it may feel as you are.

Gone From Sight:

Time To Grieve!

Grief

Grief is a response to loss. The response is emotional and can negatively affect one's physical, cognitive, behavioral, social, cultural, spiritual, and philosophical dimensions.

Name and describe the source of your grief.

Grief

_____

_____

_____

_____

_____

_____

_____

_____

_____

_____

_____

_____

_____

_____

_____

_____

_____

_____

Grief

Grief

_____

_____

_____

_____

_____

_____

_____

_____

_____

_____

_____

_____

_____

_____

_____

_____

_____

_____

Grief

_____

_____

_____

_____

_____

_____

_____

_____

_____

_____

_____

_____

_____

_____

_____

_____

_____

_____

Grief

Grief

Grief

Grief

People often say things like "this can't be happening" and often isolate themselves during this stage.

Stage 1: DENIAL

Have you experienced denial?
What did/does/could denial look like for you?

_____

_____

_____

_____

_____

_____

_____

_____

_____

_____

_____

_____

_____

_____

_____

_____

_____

_____

_____

_____

_____

Grief: Stage 1

_____

_____

_____

_____

_____

_____

_____

_____

_____

_____

_____

_____

_____

_____

_____

_____

_____

_____

_____

_____

_____

Grief: Stage 1

_____

_____

_____

_____

_____

_____

_____

_____

_____

_____

_____

_____

_____

_____

_____

_____

_____

_____

_____

Grief: Stage 1

_____

_____

_____

_____

_____

_____

_____

_____

_____

_____

_____

_____

_____

_____

_____

_____

_____

_____

_____

_____

_____

Grief: Stage 1

Grief: Stage 1

_____

_____

_____

_____

_____

_____

_____

_____

_____

_____

_____

_____

_____

_____

_____

_____

_____

_____

_____

_____

_____

_____

Grief: Stage 1

Grief: Stage 1

Grief

During this stage, in response to the pain/hurt, people often seek/desire revenge and or blame someone or themselves for not doing enough.

Stage 2: ANGER

Have you experienced denial?
What did/does/could denial look like for you?

_____

_____

_____

_____

_____

_____

_____

_____

_____

_____

_____

_____

_____

_____

_____

_____

_____

_____

_____

Grief: Stage 2

_____

_____

_____

_____

_____

_____

_____

_____

_____

_____

_____

_____

_____

_____

_____

_____

_____

_____

_____

_____

Grief: Stage 2

_____

_____

_____

_____

_____

_____

_____

_____

_____

_____

_____

_____

_____

_____

_____

_____

_____

_____

_____

_____

Grief: Stage 2

_____

_____

_____

_____

_____

_____

_____

_____

_____

_____

_____

_____

_____

_____

_____

_____

_____

_____

_____

_____

_____

_____

_____

_____

Grief: Stage 2

_____

_____

_____

_____

_____

_____

_____

_____

_____

_____

_____

_____

_____

_____

_____

_____

_____

Grief: Stage 2

_____

_____

_____

_____

_____

_____

_____

_____

_____

_____

_____

_____

_____

_____

_____

_____

_____

_____

_____

_____

Grief: Stage 2

_____

_____

_____

_____

_____

_____

_____

_____

_____

_____

_____

_____

_____

_____

_____

_____

_____

_____

_____

_____

_____

Grief: Stage 2

Grief

People will speak about trading places with another person during this stage or reflect with statements like "only if we __ then __."

Stage 3: BARGAINING

Have you bargained?
What did/does/could bargaining look like for you?

_____

_____

_____

_____

_____

_____

_____

_____

_____

_____

_____

_____

_____

_____

_____

_____

_____

Grief: Stage 3

Grief: Stage 3

_____

_____

_____

_____

_____

_____

_____

_____

_____

_____

_____

_____

_____

_____

_____

_____

_____

_____

_____

_____

_____

_____

Grief: Stage 3

_____

_____

_____

_____

_____

_____

_____

_____

_____

_____

_____

_____

_____

_____

_____

_____

_____

_____

_____

_____

_____

_____

Grief: Stage 3

_____

_____

_____

_____

_____

_____

_____

_____

_____

_____

_____

_____

_____

_____

_____

_____

_____

_____

_____

_____

_____

Grief: Stage 3

_____

_____

_____

_____

_____

_____

_____

_____

_____

_____

_____

_____

_____

_____

_____

_____

_____

_____

_____

_____

_____

_____

Grief: Stage 3

Grief: Stage 3

Grief

During this stage, emotions drop, and the sadness is palpable. Motivation is hard to generate. The days start to blend.
Grief counseling is advised!

Stage 4: DEPRESSION

Who would be your contact person on your depressed days? What is the plan to not isolate? How else can you deal with the depression?

_____

_____

_____

_____

_____

_____

_____

_____

_____

_____

_____

_____

_____

_____

_____

Grief: Stage 4

_____

_____

_____

_____

_____

_____

_____

_____

_____

_____

_____

_____

_____

_____

_____

_____

_____

_____

_____

_____

_____

_____

_____

Grief: Stage 4

_____

_____

_____

_____

_____

_____

_____

_____

_____

_____

_____

_____

_____

_____

_____

_____

_____

_____

_____

Grief: Stage 4

_____

_____

_____

_____

_____

_____

_____

_____

_____

_____

_____

_____

_____

_____

_____

_____

_____

_____

_____

_____

_____

_____

Grief: Stage 4

_____

_____

_____

_____

_____

_____

_____

_____

_____

_____

_____

_____

_____

_____

_____

_____

_____

_____

_____

_____

_____

_____

Grief: Stage 4

_____

_____

_____

_____

_____

_____

_____

_____

_____

_____

_____

_____

_____

_____

_____

_____

_____

_____

_____

_____

_____

_____

Grief: Stage 4

_____

_____

_____

_____

_____

_____

_____

_____

_____

_____

_____

_____

_____

_____

_____

_____

_____

_____

_____

_____

Grief: Stage 4

Grief

Some never reach this stage. Acceptance is when the understanding is that things cannot be changed or undone.

Stage 5: ACCEPTANCE

What have you accepted so far? What would change if you accepted that you loss someone important?

_____

_____

_____

_____

_____

_____

_____

_____

_____

_____

_____

_____

_____

_____

_____

_____

_____

Grief: Stage 5

_____

_____

_____

_____

_____

_____

_____

_____

_____

_____

_____

_____

_____

_____

_____

_____

_____

_____

_____

_____

_____

_____

Grief: Stage 5

_____

_____

_____

_____

_____

_____

_____

_____

_____

_____

_____

_____

_____

_____

_____

_____

_____

_____

_____

_____

Grief: Stage 5

_____

_____

_____

_____

_____

_____

_____

_____

_____

_____

_____

_____

_____

_____

_____

_____

_____

_____

_____

_____

_____

_____

Grief: Stage 5

_____

_____

_____

_____

_____

_____

_____

_____

_____

_____

_____

_____

_____

_____

_____

_____

_____

_____

_____

_____

_____

Grief: Stage 5

_____

_____

_____

_____

_____

_____

_____

_____

_____

_____

_____

_____

_____

_____

_____

_____

_____

_____

_____

_____

_____

Grief: Stage 5

_____

_____

_____

_____

_____

_____

_____

_____

_____

_____

_____

_____

_____

_____

_____

_____

_____

_____

_____

_____

Grief: Stage 5

Gone From Sight:
Time To Grieve!

A note from the author

It is important to grieve appropriately to reduce the chance of harsh or prolonged effects.

Condolences to you and your family.

Be well!

Thank you!

ABOUT THE AUTHOR

MJ Johnson, MS, CLC, is a psychology major with 20 years of experience in the mental health field in Massachusetts. MJ received her master's degree from the Southern University of New Hampshire and minored in business administration. MJ has worked with a wide range of clients, including individuals who have experienced trauma. MJ has also worked with people living with developmental delays, depression, anxiety, bipolar, schizophrenia, and personality disorders. Specializing in self-care and emotion awareness, MJ has partnered with multifaceted teams guided by the client*. She lives with her minor-aged children and her dog, Jax, and enjoys family time, playing board games, and dancing to unwind. For more information about MJ's work visit MJ2Coaching.academy or follow along on Instagram at @MJ2Coaching or Facebook at MJ2 Coaching

(*The term, "client" is not typically used, the term partner is preferred and more appropriate.)

www.ingramcontent.com/pod-product-compliance
Lightning Source LLC
Chambersburg PA
CBHW070334290526

45791CB00003B/1325